Record-Breaking Anima

Strongest Animals

by Lily Austen

Bullfrog Books

Ideas for Parents and Teachers

Bullfrog Books let children practice reading informational text at the earliest reading levels. Repetition, familiar words, and photo labels support early readers.

Before Reading

- Discuss the cover photo. What does it tell them?
- Look at the picture glossary together. Read and discuss the words.

Read the Book

- "Walk" through the book and look at the photos. Let the child ask questions. Point out the photo labels.
- Read the book to the child, or have him or her read independently.

After Reading

- Prompt the child to think more. Ask: There are many strong animals. Which is your favorite? Why?

Bullfrog Books are published by Jump!
5357 Penn Avenue South
Minneapolis, MN 55419
www.jumplibrary.com

Copyright © 2025 Jump! International copyright reserved in all countries. No part of this book may be reproduced in any form without written permission from the publisher.

Library of Congress Cataloging-in-Publication Data

Names: Austen, Lily, author.
Title: Strongest animals / by Lily Austen.
Description: Minneapolis, MN: Jump!, Inc., [2025]
Series: Record-breaking animals | Includes index.
Audience: Ages 5–8
Identifiers: LCCN 2023045604 (print)
LCCN 2023045605 (ebook)
ISBN 9798892131407 (hardcover)
ISBN 9798892131414 (paperback)
ISBN 9798892131421 (ebook)
Subjects: LCSH: Animals—Miscellanea—Juvenile literature. | Physiology—Juvenile literature. Muscle strength—Juvenile literature.
Classification: LCC QL49 .A843 2025 (print)
LCC QL49 (ebook)
DDC 590—dc23/eng/202312045
LC record available at https://lccn.loc.gov/2023045604
LC ebook record available at https://lccn.loc.gov/2023045605

Editor: Alyssa Sorenson
Designer: Molly Ballanger

Photo Credits: Sanit Fuangnakhon/Shutterstock, cover; Angyalosi Beata/Shutterstock, 1; daveamsler/iStock, 3; digitalskillet/iStock, 4, 23bl; Artush/iStock, 5; Antagain/iStock, 6–7; Harry Collins Photography/Shutterstock, 7; Jean-Jacques Alcalay/Biosphoto/SuperStock, 8–9; michael sheehan/Shutterstock, 10; fotoVoyager/iStock, 11, 18, 23br; GarysFRP/iStock, 12–13, 23tl; Mary Ann McDonald/Getty, 14–15; Barbara Ash/Shutterstock, 16–17 (foreground), 23tr (foreground); Mama Siba/Shutterstock, 16–17 (background), 23tr (background); MossStudio/Shutterstock, 19; lisegagne/iStock, 20–21; photomaster/Shutterstock, 22tl; Paulrommer SL/Shutterstock, 22tm; Four Oaks/Shutterstock, 22tr; Eric Isselee/Shutterstock, 22ml; Evelyn D. Harrison/Shutterstock, 22mr; GTW/Shutterstock, 22bl; Marti Bug Catcher/Shutterstock, 22br; marian78ro/Shutterstock, 24.

Printed in the United States of America at Corporate Graphics in North Mankato, Minnesota.

Table of Contents

Super Strong	4
Strongest of All	22
Picture Glossary	23
Index	24
To Learn More	24

Super Strong

How strong are you?

An ant lifts a leaf.
It is like you lifting a car!

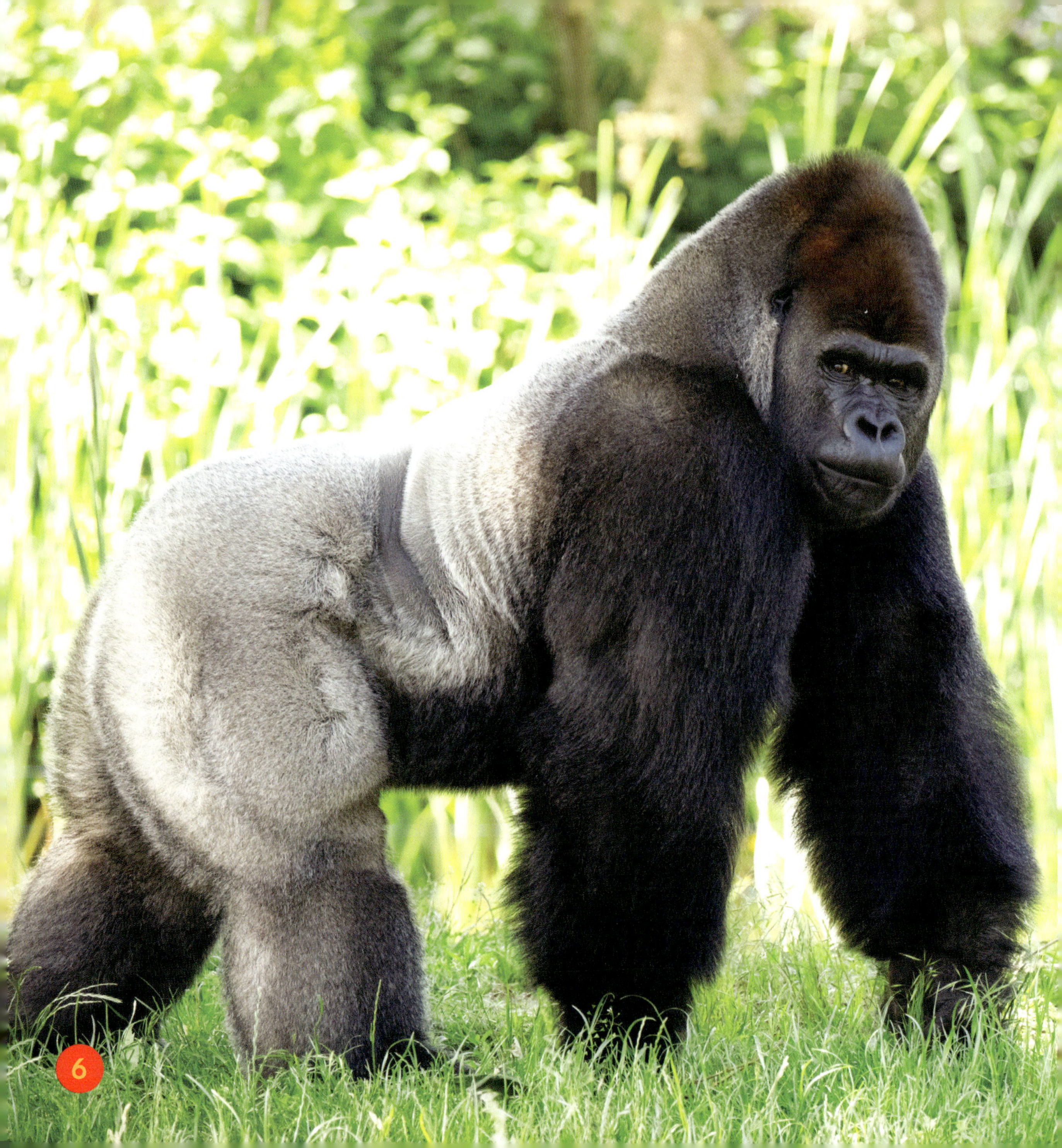

A gorilla is big.

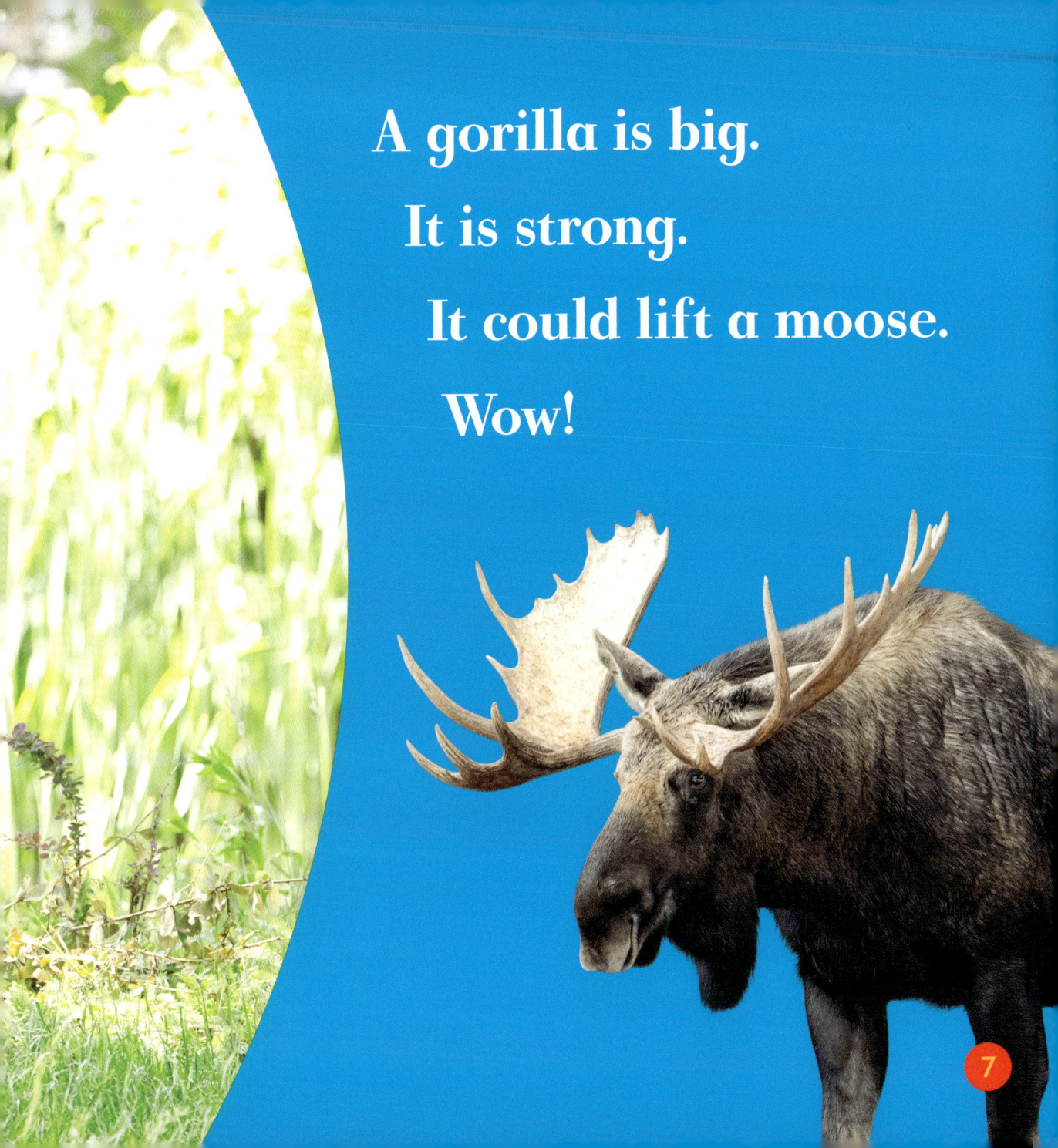

It is strong.

It could lift a moose.

Wow!

Watch out!
A croc is strong.
It has the strongest bite.
Chomp!

9

poop

What is the strongest bug?
A dung beetle!
It moves a big ball of poop.

That is like a person moving six buses!

12

A tiger is strong.

It hunts.

An eagle flies.

It is strong.

It carries a big stick.

15

mouse

Look!
A king snake is strong.
It wraps around a mouse.
It squeezes.

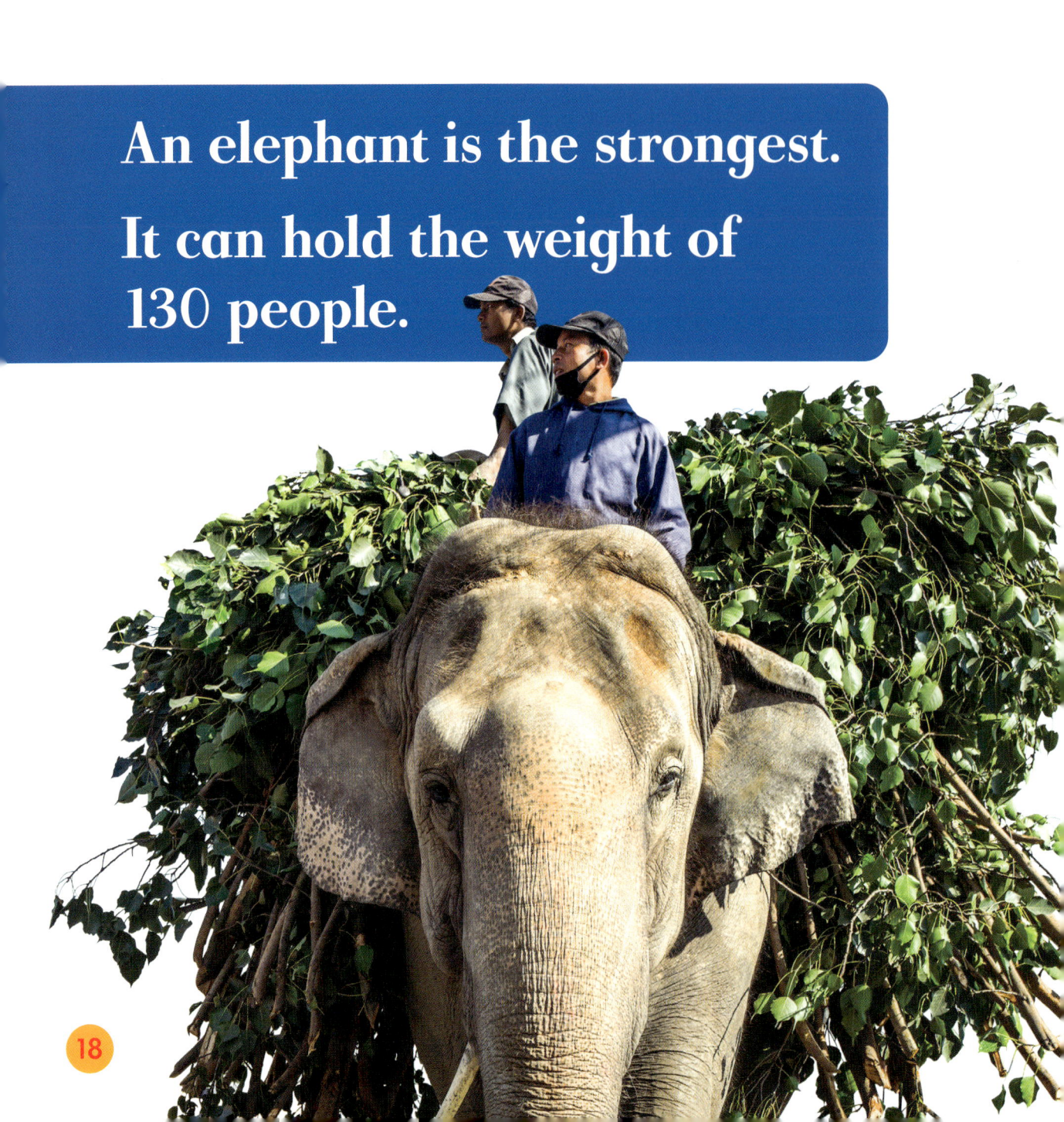

An elephant is the strongest. It can hold the weight of 130 people.

trunk

Its trunk is strong, too.
It lifts trees.

19

Have you seen a strong animal?

What did it do?

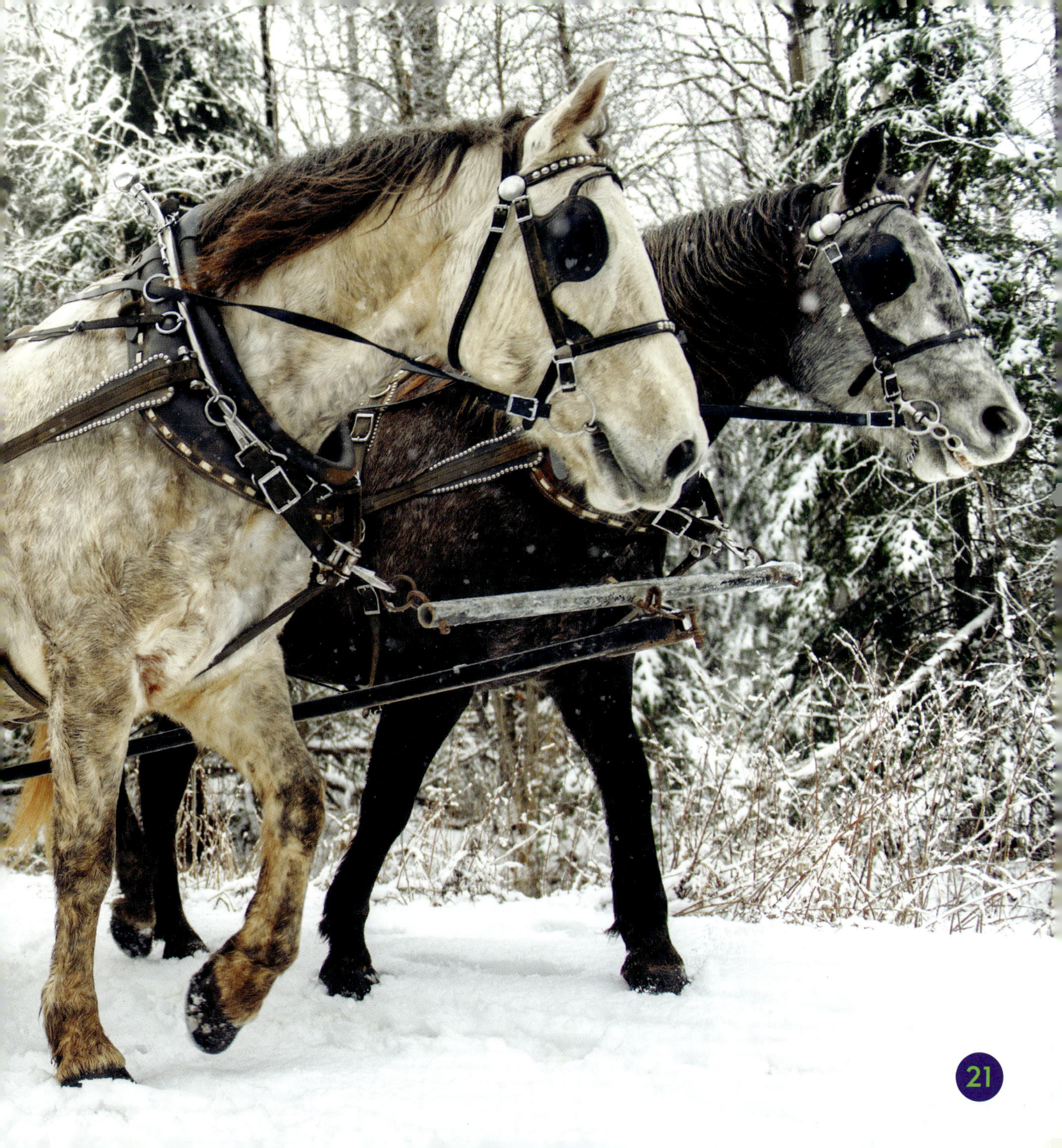

Strongest of All

What are the strongest animals? Take a look!

strongest primate: gorilla

strongest mammal: elephant

strongest bug: dung beetle

strongest big cat: tiger

strongest snake: king snake

strongest bite: Nile crocodile

strongest bird: harpy eagle

Picture Glossary

hunts
Chases and kills animals for food.

squeezes
Presses together tightly.

strong
Tough and powerful.

weight
How heavy something is.

Index

ant 5
bite 8
croc 8
dung beetle 10
eagle 14
elephant 18
gorilla 7
king snake 17
lifts 5, 7, 19
moves 10, 11
squeezes 17
tiger 13

To Learn More

Finding more information is as easy as 1, 2, 3.

❶ Go to www.factsurfer.com

❷ Enter "strongestanimals" into the search box.

❸ Choose your book to see a list of websites.